THE HOMELESS

TROUBLED

SOCIETY

THE
HOMELESS

Doug Marx

The Rourke Corporation, Inc.

The Rourke Corporation, Inc.
P.O. Box 3328, Vero Beach, FL 32964

Marx, Doug.
 The homeless / by Doug Marx.
  p. cm. — (Troubled society)
 Includes index.
 Summary: Discusses the problem of homelessness in our society, how and why people become homeless, what happens to homeless people, and possible remedies for this situation.
 ISBN 0-86593-071-6
 1. Homelessness—United States—Juvenile literature. 2. Homeless persons—United States—Juvenile literature. [1. Homelessness. 2. Homeless persons.]
I. Title. II. Series.
HV4505.M36 1990
362.5'0973—dc20   90-8819
                  CIP
                  AC

Series Editor: Gregory Lee
Editors: Elizabeth Sirimarco, Marguerite Aronowitz
Book design and production: The Creative Spark,
 Capistrano Beach, CA
Cover photograph:Tom Stack/Tom Stack & Associates
"I Ain't Got No Home"— Words and Music by Woody Guthrie
 TRO — Copyright 1961,1963 Ludlow Music, Inc., New York, NY.
 Used by permission.

THE HOMELESS

Contents

ONE

LIVING ON THE STREET

You and a friend are out running errands one day. Along the way you pass a street where dozens of scruffy-looking men and women are living on the sidewalk. Most of them are just milling about, but some are sleeping under newspapers. Others huddle in doorways or little huts they have made out of cardboard boxes.

Your friend has to return books to the library. When you get there you notice a man camped under a bush next to the building. He has made a tent out of large sheets of plastic. Around the corner, on a bench, an old woman sits talking to herself. It is a warm, sunny day, but she seems to be wearing at least three old sweaters and two tattered overcoats. Also, she has several wrinkled shopping bags in a cart beside her. They are overflowing with tattered clothes and kitchen utensils.

Thanksgiving Day, Washington, D.C. This homeless person endured four inches of snowfall.

Later, as you are coming out of the grocery store, a man in need of a shave asks you for some spare change. Perhaps you give him a quarter. As you leave the parking lot you notice another man looking through one of the store's big dumpsters.

On the way home you see a couple of other men rummaging through garbage cans. Sometimes this happens at the park near your house. They usually carry plastic bags or push shopping carts that they fill with empty bottles and cans. They will make a couple of dollars turning in the empties at a store or redemption center. There is an old station wagon parked nearby. It's crammed full of papers and blankets because a family with two kids is living in it. You realize that you see people like this every-

where you go. Maybe you wonder who they are and where they come from.

Although they all have names and are people like everyone else, these individuals are called the *homeless*. They are men, women and children who are so poor and down on their luck they cannot afford a house or apartment, a place they can call their own. They come from all walks of life, all races and religions. Many of them are hard-working people who lost their jobs during the economic changes of the 1980s and were not able to find other employment. Many more are those who were already poor and for whom the past decade has proved catastrophic. Among the homeless you will also find many people who have mental illnesses. These illnesses make it difficult, if not sometimes impossible, for these people to hold steady jobs.

Estimates vary about the number of homeless people in the United States today. In 1984, the Department of Housing and Urban Development estimated that there were about 350,000 homeless people. This figure was based on the number of people who slept in temporary shelters every night. These shelters might be church basements or old hotels that have been converted for use by the homeless. They are always full to overflowing, and many people are turned away every day. Many more homeless people have given up trying to find a sheltered bed each night. Instead, they simply sleep on the streets, under bridges, in parks—wherever they can. Until the taking of the 1990 Census, the government has never tried to get an accurate count of homeless people who live in and out of shelters.

Homeless people often must search through garbage dumpsters to find warm clothing, junk to sell—and sometimes their next meal.

It will take some time for the 1990 Census figures to be made official. During the 1980s, reports provided by private social agencies and other groups who work with the homeless suggest that there are as many as three million homeless people in this country. These advocacy groups claim that there are many more homeless people than those who sleep in shelters.

In large cities such as New York, which has an

estimated 70,000 homeless people, thousands set up tents and cardboard boxes in public parks. Others sleep side by side on city sidewalks. In Washington, D.C., many homeless people huddle in the streets just a few blocks from the White House. In the winter, some try to keep warm by propping up their huts and tents over steam vents in the streets. Others live in abandoned, rat- and cockroach-infested buildings without running water, heat and electricity. Some spend their winter nights trying to keep warm by standing around metal barrels in which they burn trash.

Wherever the homeless sleep, this much is sure: their plight is one of the biggest problems facing America today. Whether they number 350,000 or 3,000,000, the number is too high. Homelessness has affected a broad cross-section of our society. In terms of the harm to human lives, or in terms of the social and economic cost to society, the toll is great.

There have always been homeless people, but during the last ten years their numbers have increased dramatically. You can see them in the city, the suburbs, and the country. Because there are so many of them, the homeless have also been called the "visible poor."

Who Are They?

The homeless in America today come from all kinds of backgrounds. Although surveys vary in counting the actual number of homeless people, they generally agree on the kinds of individuals who make up the homeless population. *Intact families*, which consist of a father, mother and children, comprise 20 percent of the homeless population. If these families have two or more children, then at least 10 percent of the homeless are children under 16 years of age. A small percentage of homeless people are teenage runaways.

Single women comprise another 20 percent of the homeless. These women often can't work because they have children to care for, and they can't afford to send them to daycare. Nearly one-third of the homeless population are women and their young children.

The remaining 60 percent of the homeless are lone adult males. They tend to be young men in their late 30s to early 40s. Nearly one-third of these men—or 20 percent of the entire homeless population--are veterans of our armed services. It is sometimes assumed that the majority of these men are veterans of the Vietnam War, but this is not the case. Most homeless veterans are men who enlisted during the 1970s or 1980s. Quite a few are from troubled or poor backgrounds. They might have joined the armed services to learn job skills, or were high school dropouts who intended to finish their education in the service. Unfortunately, after leaving the service they found jobs hard to come by.

Roughly 40 percent of the homeless population can be described as non-elderly, non-veteran men. This is an extremely general category. Some are college educated, some are high school dropouts. Some are fathers, some are not. Some have drug and alcohol problems, some do not. As is true of all the homeless, these men come from broad economic and racial backgrounds.

Because no one has tried to conduct a proper national survey to find out about the homeless before the 1990 Census, there is no real data currently avail-

Holding her wet clothes under a hand dryer, a woman does her laundry in this ladies room in a New York City subway station.

able about their lives. What we know about the home-less is sketchy. A survey conducted by a recent U.S. Conference of Mayors, however, revealed that approx-imately 25 percent of homeless people have full- or part-time jobs. Other studies, such as one conducted by the National Institute for Mental Health, indicate that as many as one-half to two-thirds of homeless peo-ple have completed high school.

It has also been noticed that many homeless suf-fer from moderate-to-severe psychiatric disorders. Some of them cannot get the medical help they need because of budget cutbacks in community health resource centers. Usually these people pose no threat of danger to themselves or others. Although they are not ill enough to be hospitalized, they do not have the necessary skills to take care of themselves.

Very few of the homeless are elderly. Federal programs such as Social Security and Medicare have eased the economic burdens of many senior citizens, allowing them to maintain a modest standard of liv-ing. In 1988 the average age of a homeless person was estimated to be 34, which means that most homeless people are part of the large generation of Americans born after World War II called the "baby boomers."

TWO

HOW THEY BECAME HOMELESS

Imagine that one morning over breakfast your father tells you that he has lost his job. The company he works for has laid off many employees. He tells you that it will be hard to make ends meet for a time. He says that money for fun things such as ice cream and movies will be in short supply, because every dollar must go to pay the rent. Your mother might work, too, but her income alone will not be enough to maintain your family's *standard of living*. Your standard of living means the things you can or cannot afford in terms of the money you make. Rich people are said to have high standards of living. Poor people have low ones.

Every day your father looks for work, but there aren't any jobs to be found. Your father might have spent his life as a steelworker, for example, and now finds himself untrained for other occupations. Worse, many companies are going out of business altogether. The entire country is in the middle of an economic "slump" or "recession," and work is hard to come by. Your family meets to decide how to deal with this difficult time. You discover that some of your friends' fathers have been laid off too.

According to government figures, in 1984 the United States unemployment rate was 12 percent. (Surveys conducted by private research groups often put that figure at 16 to 18 percent.) This means that three to four million men and women were out of work. In a year such as 1984 it would've been normal for your father to join hundreds of others standing in line at employment windows, waiting for one job opening.

Many Americans filed bankruptcy in the 1980s.

Evicted with nowhere to go.

Many lost their homes to banks and other lending agencies because they could not pay the mortgage. Many more were evicted from their apartments because they could not pay the rent. From the timber mill-towns of the Pacific Northwest to the farms of the Midwest to the factories in the Northeast, millions found themselves unemployed.

An example of mass unemployment can be found in the city of Flint, Michigan. For over 50 years most of the residents of Flint worked for the local General Motors Corporation automotive plants. The economic welfare of the whole city depended on a single company. Then, during the 1980s, General Motors closed down its plants and moved them to foreign countries where it was less expensive to operate.

In Flint, a town with a population of approximately 140,000, over 30,000 people were laid off. To make matters worse, these people had no hope of getting their old jobs back or finding work they had been trained to do. They not only found themselves out of work, but unskilled for new kinds of work as well. Many people left Flint. Between 1980 and 1989, more than 20,000 moved away. Yet this unemployment crisis was repeated in many cities throughout the United States.

Now let's go back to our make-believe predicament, where your family is trying to make it on only one income. Your parents manage to keep things together, at least for awhile. Your father is eligible to receive *unemployment insurance* from the state government, which might last six months to a year, but no longer. The unemployment insurance is much less than the salary your father made when he was working. Your parents might also apply for *food stamps* issued by the federal government (coupons that can be used to buy groceries). Still, your father's monthly unemployment check and the food stamps will not be enough for your family to live on.

Your parents will probably have to use up their savings. Credit card charges and other bills will add up and have to be paid. Your father might leave home for long periods of time to look for work in other parts of the country. If he does not have any luck, he might tell you it is time for your family to find a cheaper place to live.

Inexpensive apartments or houses to rent are

difficult to find because so many people—people just like you and your family—are in need of them. If your father's unemployment insurance runs out before he finds a new job, you and your family might be forced to live in shelters. You and your mother are eligible for economic assistance, such as the government's Aid to Families with Dependent Children program. But in order for your mother to receive this money, your father must first move out. In other words, your family must break up. The government will not provide welfare assistance to families who have an able-bodied man in the house, no matter how severe the unemployment problem.

Although this story is only make-believe, this type of situation is all too true for many families nowadays. Remember that 20 percent of the homeless population consists of families living together. These are people who choose to remain together as a family, regardless of the hardships and the lack of welfare assistance.

It often is difficult for families to stay together even in the best of economic times. Joblessness, the main reason for homelessness, can make keeping a family together almost impossible. A job and a decent income give people a sense of future and hope. Without money, life becomes difficult and people often become frustrated and angry. Sometimes the strain breaks up marriages.

If a divorced father is unemployed, the mother cannot count on alimony or child support money from him. That mother becomes a single woman with children. Because women in America are (on the average) paid only two-thirds of what men receive for the

Many homeless people have trouble looking after themselves because of mental or physical illnesses.

same work, times can be tough for women—even those having good jobs. If she is lucky, a mother might have relatives willing to help her out. If not, and if there is no other solution, mothers and their children join the growing ranks of the homeless.

Twenty percent of the homeless are accounted for by single women with and without children. Many of these women are divorced, or victims of domestic violence and abuse. Although there are homes for battered women, most of them have long waiting lists. There is just not enough help available for those who need it.

An even greater percentage of homeless people come from poor backgrounds. These are people who were already so poor that hard economic times forced them to live in the streets. Many once lived in "tenement" apartments, or other kinds of low-income housing. In the 1980s many old houses and urban apartment buildings were bought by real estate developers who fixed them up and rented them at higher prices. When low-income people have to find another place to live, often there is none to be found.

Some homeless people are ill and cannot help themselves, at least without the help of others. When experts at Johns Hopkins University in Maryland studied the homeless population of Baltimore in 1989, they found that 42 percent of the men and 49 percent of the women suffered from major mental illnesses such as schizophrenia and dementia. An *additional* 30 percent of the men and 46 percent of the women suffered from other mental disorders.

It was late in the 1970s when various mental health organizations decided that people with moderate mental disabilities should be allowed to live in mainstream society. Many people were released from mental institutions who were unable to fend for themselves. This plan, called *de-institutionalization*, would have been successful if federal and state governments had fulfilled their promises to build "halfway" houses and community resource centers where these people could go for shelter, counseling and medical help. Unfortunately, the government failed to provide any place for them to go to be treated. As a result, they were left to wander the streets.

We have discussed how unemployment and the problems of the mentally ill have contributed to the homeless situation, but homelessness can seldom be blamed on one or two causes. Another important eco-

C.C. Bruno: Portrait Of A Homeless Man

Ever since he returned to the United States from the Korean War in the 1950s, C.C. Bruno has made his living as an agricultural worker in California's fertile Imperial Valley. But as Bruno says in an article he wrote for *The Humanist* magazine, "In 1986, I joined the ranks of the homeless, forced there by the influx of the new and younger agricultural workers admitted to the United States under the Immigration and Naturalization Reform Act of 1986."

The Immigration and Naturalization Act allowed foreign workers or "illegal aliens" from countries such as Mexico to become United States citizens. Though this legislation was designed to ease the hardships of farm laborers living in migrant shacks, it had the effect of allowing hundreds of thousands of foreign workers into this country. These workers took the jobs formerly held by Americans.

In his article, which is called "Why I Am Homeless," Bruno notes that many of these newcomers become homeless. "They have found out how much easier it is to live on the street in the United States than in their native Mexico," he says. Worse, these people use up the services set up for American citizens who have fallen on hard times.

Unable to make ends meet working minimum-wage jobs 40 hours a week, Bruno started living in city parks. "When I go north in California," he explains, "work is scarce and I have to rely on soup kitchens and shelters. To me, shelter is most important. I can usually find something to eat behind food markets by going through dumpsters for discarded vegetables or by picking up aluminum cans and selling them for a few cents to buy a loaf of bread and some bologna."

Pointing out that a lack of low-cost housing is the fundamental problem for the homeless individual, Bruno cites the recent decline of affordable hotel rooms. Bruno also takes issue with those who think the answer to homelessness is building government-subsidized housing for families. "What are the people doing wrong who are talking about providing housing?" he asks. "They are overlooking the individuals out there. They say 'Help them to help themselves.' The majority of the people on the street are not families but single people. They are overlooking that."

nomic factor has to do with sharp budget cuts in social spending. For example, tax dollars once used for government support of child daycare and food stamps programs have been decreased to cut government spending.

A 1987 report from the Census Bureau estimates that 25 million Americans live below the "poverty level." This means that a family of four lives on less than $9,000 per year. Many of these people rely on some form of government aid to get by. The money they save on groceries by using food stamps, for example, helps to pay the rent. When this kind of government support is cut back, sometimes the rent doesn't get paid and families have to move out.

Another serious economic factor that contributes to the plight of the homeless is the shortage of low-income housing. Low-income housing generally means apartments that are built with tax dollars. The government keeps the rent prices low, so people without much money can afford them. In 1981, the government spent $32.2 billion on low-income housing projects. By 1988, that budget had been cut to $7.1 billion. Ironically, at the same time that fewer and fewer apartments were being built, more and more people were becoming homeless.

During the last decade, the United States lost *one-half* of its single-room occupancy hotels (hotels that rent single rooms with a tiny bathroom, or maybe one bathroom for a whole floor). The rents are low. Ideally, one of these rooms is suitable for just one person. Many men who are now homeless used to live in these hotels. Very poor, large families also would cram into one-room lodgings, and they still do if they can find them. The few single-room occupancy hotels that remain are often the last resort of the poor. Without them, these people have nowhere else to go but the streets.

What is the bottom line? Over the last 10 years, 2.5 million units of low-income housing have vanished. Some have closed down and stand empty. Others have been torn down. Many others "vanish" in the sense that they are fixed up and rented out again at higher prices.

The causes of homelessness are all interrelated. Economically, homelessness involves unemployment and federal budget cuts in social services and low-income housing. In terms of human lives, homelessness is often a mental health problem, a substance abuse problem, a family problem. It is also a problem for all of us to help solve.

One reason the homeless problem in America continues to be so large is that society is not doing much about it. Charitable organizations who help the homeless receive less and less money each year, despite the fact that most of America is quite prosperous. National opinion polls indicate that there is a current trend of thinking that the homeless are "lazy bums," "freeloaders" and "drug addicts." This attitude wrongly implies that a homeless person is not worthy of help.

Studies show that as many as half of the homeless do suffer from some kind of drug or alcohol abuse. There is little evidence, however, to show that these people became homeless *because* of their substance abuse problems. Many believe that the opposite is more likely, that these people probably began to

When asked why she slept in a phone booth, this woman answered,
"Because there's a light on at night."

abuse drugs and alcohol *after*—not before—they became homeless. In today's society there is a high degree of drug and alcohol abuse overall. People who have jobs and health insurance can afford treatment for addiction to smoking, drinking and cocaine. Homeless people have very limited access to this kind of help.

Other people suggest that homeless people "choose" to be homeless. These arguments are, by and large, unsupported by the evidence and common sense. Homeless people lead desperate, lonely, needy lives, and it is unkind to suggest they are on the streets by choice. Although a small percentage of homeless people might prefer living on the streets to working, the majority do not. They want a job and a home just like anyone else. It is wrong to penalize those who are truly in need of help because of a few who might be homeless by choice.

THREE

PROBLEMS OF THE HOMELESS

The difficulties encountered by the homeless go far beyond those of finding food and shelter. Imagine waking each day in a strange place, not knowing where your next meal will come from, or where you'll sleep that night. After days, weeks, months—and sometimes years—of struggling to survive with no end in sight, hopelessness sets in. The future seems not only bleak but nonexistent. If you believe that society does not care for you, you might stop caring about yourself.

Within the homeless population, perhaps no group is more tragic than that of the homeless intact family. Particularly hard hit are the children. Studies on the children of homeless families reveal that they are many times more likely to become sick or suffer other physical disorders. This is because good, nutritious food and clean, healthful living conditions are not a regular part of a homeless child's daily life.

A young homeless person is also at tremendous risk because of the danger and violence that often goes with living on the streets. The homeless often live in poor areas where the crime rate is high. Going to school or walking to the store might mean encountering drug pushers and gang members.

The homeless children have little if any control over what is happening to them. They are frequently depressed and sad. Some of them suffer from learning disabilities. Because of the unstable nature of their lives, most of them will not graduate from high school. Indeed, for many homeless youngsters, going to school is just about impossible. Without help and a decent education, there is

The South Bronx in New York, where empty buildings are everywhere—abandoned, gutted, condemned or in disrepair. Many homeless people live in such squalid dwellings.

a good chance that homelessness will be their fate for their entire lives.

Adult homeless people are beset with the same physical and psychological difficulties as the young. Approximately one-third suffer from mental illness. One-half suffer from drug and alcohol-related problems. Still, whatever the impact that mental illness, drugs and alcohol have on the homeless, they are secondary to economic factors. Once a person becomes homeless, it is very difficult to find work and save enough to start over.

930063

Imagine that you have lost your job and been forced to live on the streets. You'd sleep in shelters, doorways or city parks and eat in "soup kitchens." Like other homeless people, you have lost your identity. You have no address, no phone number, no checking or savings account, no credit, no job references—things considered to be minimum requirements in finding a job and getting a new start in life.

Let us also suppose that you do find work—most likely a minimum-wage job that pays $4.25 an hour. If you work full-time (40 hours per week), your monthly income after taxes will be a little more than $500. Even the cheapest apartment or hotel room usually will cost $250 to $300 per month. In most cases, the landlord will ask you for either a rent deposit or an entire month's rent in advance. It will be very difficult to save up enough money to rent living space. If you have small children who will need to be cared for while you work, the situation becomes nearly impossible, because child care is expensive.

Children and families make up an ever increasing portion of homeless people. This child was lucky—he now has a home.

To make matters worse, without a permanent address, you might not be eligible for some kinds of government assistance. Nor will your $4.25-an-hour job probably include such things as medical insurance or sick leave time. This means that any time you become ill and have to go to the doctor, not only will you lose the money you would have made by working, the doctor bills will take up what little money you have left.

The sad fact is that even if a homeless person does minimum wage work, the money will not be

enough to help him or her out of their homeless situation. True, they can often find short-term relief in the way of shelters, soup kitchens and free or "sliding scale" medical clinics where patients pay only what they can afford. But most of these social agencies are too under-funded and under-staffed to handle the number of people who need their help. The basic fact of life for most homeless people is their lack of physical, financial, emotional and spiritual support. They are profoundly alone, living without any sense of family, neighborhood or community.

Where They Live

Homeless people live wherever they can. From government data we know that roughly 350,000 homeless people sleep in shelters every night. Shelters are generally run by city governments or nonprofit church and social service groups. Some shelters look like army barracks. They have one large room with rows of cots. When the doors are opened, these beds are quickly taken each day. In most shelters, a homeless person can only stay for one night. He or she must then give someone else a turn. Shelters that take in women with children, however, allow stays of up to a month.

Some churches convert their basements into shelters for the homeless. Others provide weekly meals such as pancake breakfasts and spaghetti dinners. But most shelters—especially in large cities—are "welfare hotels." These are old hotels that have been converted for use by the homeless. The rooms are small, run-down, and furnished with only the bare necessities.

Civic leaders have begun recently to close

down these barracks and welfare hotel shelters because they understand that even with a shelter, a homeless person is still homeless. They want to move homeless people out of shelters and into apartments. They want to build more low-income housing to give homeless people a sense of having roots—a regular routine and a place to stay. This is a good idea, but some lawmakers want to close down the shelters even though low-income housing is not yet widely available.

Homeless people must get by any way they can. For most, this means living on the streets, right out in the open. In cities on the west coast, where the weather is temperate, many homeless people camp out. In Portland, Oregon, a census taker counting the homeless found a man living inside a huge blackberry patch. It was both his home and his secret hiding spot. A visitor to New York will see whole city blocks lined with people lying on cardboard boxes that are being used as mattresses. Doorways and under bridges are useful places to sleep because they provide cover from the rain or snow. In good weather, many homeless people sleep in city parks or squares.

In recent years, some homeless people have started fixing up and living in abandoned buildings. This is called "squatting." It is against the law, but they are doing it anyway. There are empty buildings in every city. A lot of them are in bad shape, but others can be made livable with a little work. Many times these buildings are owned by the government. Frustrated because government cannot help them, these people are helping themselves. The irony, of course, is that they are breaking the law for doing something constructive about their situation.

Lashanda Daniels: Portrait Of A Homeless Child

As a seventh-grader at Boston's James P. Timilty School, 12-year old Lashanda Daniels entered and won a city-wide essay contest on the theme of the homeless. Lashanda didn't have to do any research for her essay because she and her family had lived for five months in a shelter.

"Being homeless is not having your own home," Lashanda wrote, "but to those that are homeless it is more than that. It is a situation that is caused by some unknown circumstance that renders them helpless and causes a feeling of insecurity. Being homeless makes finding yourself and deciding what you want to be in life a major problem."

Lashanda and her family—which includes four brothers—became homeless after they moved to Detroit in search of a better life. Her mother, Carolyn, spent all of her savings to make the trip, but when they got there they found a drug and gang situation worse than the one they'd left behind in Boston. Returning to

Boston without any money, they learned that they were no longer eligible for housing assistance. The family had to move into a shelter. Five months later they were fortunate enough to find a state-subsidized apartment.

In her essay, Lashanda talked about how it felt to be homeless. "First you hate yourself for having to be in this predicament," she said. "Then that feeling of hate spreads towards those around you. You find yourself being jealous of those who have a home and you feel as if everyone looks down on you."

Having been homeless herself, Lashanda was able to convey her thoughts with honesty and compassion. In fact, her essay not only won the Boston prize, but the story of her success later appeared in *People* magazine. "I wanted to tell people it's not an easy feeling [being homeless]," she told an interviewer. "I wanted to tell them to bear with the homeless. Don't put them down. It might not be their fault. It can feel very hopeless."

Juan Alvarez lives in a cardboard shack next to an elevated highway in New York City. Keeping warm in freezing temperatures is a constant battle for many homeless people.

One thing is certain about where the homeless live: wherever it is, they are not welcome. Police "sweeps" of homeless camps under city bridges and in parks are routine. There are sound reasons for these actions, however, among them the fact that these camps are often unsanitary. In Tompkins Square Park in New York, for example, thousands of homeless people set up an encampment of huts and plastic tents. The police were called in to remove them because their presence discourages other people from using the park. The police evicted the homeless, with force if necessary, and had the huts and tents hauled to the garbage dump. In 1988 and 1989, these confrontations between the police and the homeless caused riots, and many people were hurt.

In Portland, Oregon, many businesses have put sprinklers on their roofs, turning them on whenever homeless people sit on the sidewalk. In Atlanta, Georgia, businessmen who stay in the hotel district want the city to call this area a "hospitality zone" for tourists and keep homeless people out. People in other cities are also doing this kind of thing. For example, they want to close off shopping areas to homeless people who *panhandle*—asking shoppers for money. Some people want laws that forbid begging and panhandling. To date, the courts have disagreed whether laws like this are unconstitutional. Asking for money, some argue, is a form of expression guaranteed by the First Amendment. But at least one New York appeals court ruled in 1990 that panhandling was a "menace to the common good." It remains an undecided issue.

FOUR

AN OLD PROBLEM

Historically, America is a country where the homeless of the world have come to find a home. The United States is a nation built by people who left their native lands to escape religious and political persecution, war and poverty. Americans are proud of their immigrant heritage. We call our country the "melting pot" because people of many different races and nationalities have come here to live and make a better life for themselves. On July 4, 1986, we celebrated the 100th anniversary of the Statue of Liberty. "Miss Liberty" is a symbol of our national belief that this is the land of opportunity for everyone. This country has provided food, shelter, and the opportunity for a better life to millions, yet poverty and homelessness have always been and continue to be problems.

During the early 1900s, millions of European immigrants settled in large cities such as New York and Chicago. Working conditions were severe, and people were very poor. Men, women, and children worked in factories and sweatshops 12 to 16 hours a day, six days a week, for pennies. Large families crammed themselves into one or two-room tenement buildings. The slums had names such as Hell's Kitchen, Poverty Gap and Bandit's Roost. Public education for children was virtually unheard of. There were no laws designed to protect children from life in the sweatshops.

In those days, people without work or a roof over their head were called *vagrants* and *paupers*, rather than homeless. They were considered lazy, no-good weaklings. Many were thrown into jail. In 1904, in a famous book called *Poverty*, a social worker named Robert Hunter declared that ten million Americans lived in poverty. Of

A shantytown from the 1930s. "Okies"—migrant workers from plains states—traveled to other states to pick crops for meager wages.

those ten million, four million were considered vagrants and paupers, or homeless.

These terrible conditions prevailed for the next 30 years, and then they got worse. The stock market crash of 1929 heralded the Great Depression. In 1929, America--and most of the western world for that matter--experienced an economic disaster. In a sense, the entire country went bankrupt. By 1932, one out of every four American workers was unemployed.

Like today's homeless, these people could not earn enough to pay for rent and food. They lived in the streets or rambled around the country looking for work, sleeping in "shanty towns," "hobo jungles," and tar-paper cities called "Hoovervilles." Hoovervilles were named after Herbert Hoover, who was president when the Great Depression began. It was a common sight in big cities to see thousands of people hanging around soup kitchens or standing in bread lines, waiting for something to eat. A popular song of the times was "Buddy, Can You Spare a Dime?"

The Great Depression lasted 10 years. At the same time nature contributed more misfortune. To add to the misery of farmers, dust storms swirled over plains states such as Oklahoma from 1934 through 1936, ruining millions of acres of farmland. What had once been America's "Farm Belt" suddenly became the "Dust Bowl." Tens of thousands of families and farm workers left their barren farms behind and headed west, mostly to California, looking for work. Others fled north and northeast to large manufacturing cities, which only added to the unemployment problems there.

The Dust Bowl homeless were called "Okies"—a nickname they did not like—because so many came from Oklahoma. In *The Grapes of Wrath*, by John Steinbeck, the homeless Joad family travels from Oklahoma to California with their meager belongings piled high on an old battered pickup truck. Steinbeck portrayed the "Okies" as proud people trying to better themselves. The movie of the same name graphically portrayed the hard lives of these unfortunate people.

It was during the Great Depression that

During the Great Depression, thousands of unemployed people stood in line at "rescue missions" such as this to receive a bowl of soup and a piece of bread.

President Franklin Roosevelt instituted many social reforms that we take for granted today. His "New Deal" social policies included Social Security benefits and the beginning of unemployment insurance. In 1938, the Fair Labor Standards Act was made into law, which lowered the hours per week a person could be made to work and, eventually, brought an end to the horrors of child labor.

The Great Depression did not really come to an end until the outbreak of World War II in 1941, when America became the "arsenal for democracy." Millions of men, many unemployed, either enlisted or were drafted into the armed services. Others, including many women, went to work in factories that produced the guns, tanks, and planes needed for the war effort.

When peace was achieved in 1945, America was on its way to economic recovery. Until the 1980s, most Americans had a job and a roof over their head. There were a few spells of large unemployment, particularly during the mid-1970s after the Vietnam War. But the truth is, poverty and unemployment have remained facts of life for millions, especially minority groups such as blacks and Hispanics. What makes the homeless problem today unique is that it is so visible. Homeless people are everywhere. This has not happened since the Great Depression.

Homelessness Around The World

Homelessness has taken several forms and has been a major social problem throughout recorded human history. The fact that millions of people do not have adequate food or shelter is neither new nor America's problem alone.

One major cause of universal homelessness is war. Wars occur for many reasons—racial tension, boundary disputes, social and economic injustice, and religious intolerance. Whatever the reason, innocent people are always caught in the crossfire. Most of them are women, children, and the elderly. People who are driven from their homes by war are called refugees. The term refugees was coined during the

American Civil War to describe the thousands of non-military people who were victims of that bloody dispute.

Another principal cause of world homelessness is natural disasters. Earthquakes, floods and droughts have the power to reduce communities to rubble or ghost towns, leaving many dead and many more homeless. In the days of ancient Rome, the entire city of Pompeii was destroyed when the volcano called Mount Vesuvius exploded and buried everything for miles around it.

In recent times a volcano called Mount St. Helens erupted in the Pacific Northwest of the United States. The force of that explosion destroyed homes for miles around, and the lava dust that drifted through the air was so thick it drove people out of their communities. The San Francisco earthquake of October 1989 crumbled bridges, apartment buildings, and private residences, killing some people and leaving many more without shelter.

There is currently mass starvation and homelessness in the drought-striken area of Ethiopia. For over a decade the once lush and fertile pasture and farmlands of Ethiopia have suffered from a severe lack of rain, which has turned the ground to dust—just as in Oklahoma in the Great Depression. Millions of Ethiopians wander through this desert in search of water, food and shelter.

Homelessness is a complex situation often caused by more than one factor. In a so-called "Third World" (or underdeveloped) country, it often happens that political turmoil, widespread hunger, and natural catastrophes combine to create mass homelessness.

The nation of Nicaragua is a good example of

this. Although rich in natural resources, the vast majority of Nicaraguans are very poor. For several decades they were forced to live under the dictatorial rule of the Somoza family. In 1979 the people of Nicaragua revolted, overthrowing the powerful Somozas. Soon thereafter a civil war began that left tens of thousands dead and even more homeless. To make matters worse, in 1984 Nicaragua was devastated by an earthquake so severe that the country has yet to recover from the damage. On top of all of this, the United States government placed an economic embargo on Nicaragua, which means that the U.S. would not do business with Nicaragua.

There are several Third World countries in which a great many people suffer and are homeless. Some of them are just south of the United States, including Mexico, Guatemala and El Salvador. Cambodia and Vietnam are two countries in Southeast Asia that have tremendous refugee and homeless problems. Recent reports from the United Nations Children's Fund (UNICEF) estimate that tens of millions of people in the world are homeless. Most of them live in refugee camps set up by such organizations as the International Red Cross.

Another cause of national and international homelessness is that of overpopulation. The earth might seem large and unlimited, but the natural resources needed to sustain human life are finite. This problem becomes clear when there are too many people living in one place. Although many countries are overpopulated, the most frequently mentioned example is India. If you were to visit Calcutta, India's capital city, you would see millions of thin, sickly people who sleep in the streets and beg for food.

Last, but not least, are the economic factors involved in world homelessness. For instance, some workers in Third World countries make less than one dollar a day. Also, the economic systems they work under are usually inflationary. Economic inflation means that things get more and more expensive, but people's earning power stays the same. In some countries, a half gallon of milk or a dozen eggs might cost a whole week's pay.

Americans have tried to help the world's homeless through economic aid and programs such as the Peace Corps. A sad irony of this generosity is that Americans often spend more money on other nations' problems than on their own.

FIVE

THE PRICE OF HOMELESSNESS

Measuring the economic impact of homelessness is difficult because we do not yet have accurate statistics. Figures available from individual cities, however, can give some idea of the basic cost of homelessness. For example, in Washington, D.C., it costs the city taxpayers $30 million per year to provide minimum shelter for 26,000 homeless people.

In Seattle, taxpayers and social agencies spend $6 million each year to provide 19,000 housing units, yet 2,500 people still sleep in the streets every night. In New York City, the Human Resources Administration spends about $330 million each year to combat homelessness. Nationally, President Bush's early 1990 budget plan calls for $728 million to aid the homeless. These figures amount to a lot of money but, in a sense, they are insufficient to handle the problem. Compared to the billions of tax dollars spent on defense and foreign aid, they are very small. One Stealth bomber, for instance, costs $750 million to build. And it is difficult to understand why our government is willing to spend so much money on hunger and homelessness around the world, yet so little on those who live in our midst.

A sign on this Harlem marquee promises renewal and civic improvement. The reality in so many American cities today is that there are no public funds to help revive blighted urban neighborhoods.

The figures given above are also small when compared to the amount of money it will take to correct the homeless problem. Nobody knows how much that will be, but advocates for the homeless say that what we spend now is miniscule.

A March 1990 study in Portland, Oregon showed that it would cost $443 million to build the low-income housing needed to eliminate homelessness there. And Portland has only about one-tenth of the population of New York City. Yet the report called for more money than New York City is spending today! No one in Portland knows where the $443 million will come from. That is a staggering sum to raise for a city with a metropolitan population of just one million people. Worse still is knowing that unless this kind of money is spent now to build housing, it will cost much more in the future.

Even without new housing, money is needed continually to try to help the homeless. All social problems have "hidden costs." For example, when experts talk about the dangers of alcoholism, they also talk about the millions of dollars lost to the economy because alcoholics miss a lot of work. There are a lot of hidden economic costs caused by homelessness. The problems of the homeless affect many of society's institutions such as the educational system, the police departments, and the courts. They put a strain on already over-burdened public health systems. Whatever the problem of homelessness costs society today, it will most certainly cost more tomorrow.

This is equally true when it comes to understanding the "social costs" of homelessness. The value of human life and how we feel about our society cannot always be measured in dollars. No one but the homeless themselves can measure the cost of their misery. Our consciences might tell us that it is unjust for people to have to live on streets and in alleyways. Our consciences might teach us to have compassion for

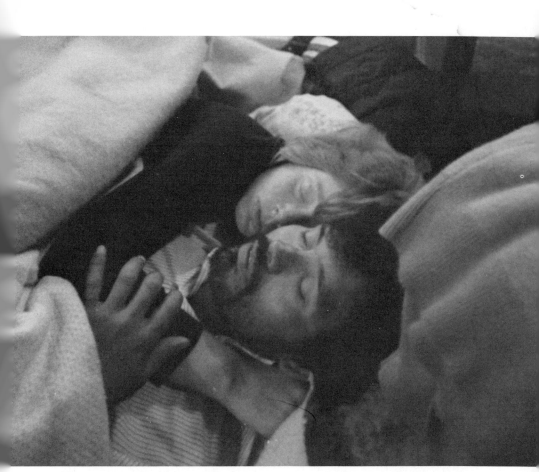

This couple huddles together for warmth as they sleep in the council chambers of the Los Angeles City Hall. An unusual week of cold weather convinced the city to open the facility to homeless people for several nights.

poor people. We may feel the desire to help them. But only those who live with the hunger and broken dreams can tell us the true cost.

When society is confronted with a problem like homelessness, it must decide how to handle it. This is the way society as a whole expresses its values. In the United States today, most Americans are genuinely concerned about homeless people. At the same time, many do not want to accept any responsibility for solving this problem. They want the problem to go away without their spending any money or getting involved.

The social cost in this instance is a kind of hypocrisy. The United States is one of the wealthiest, most powerful countries on earth. It is ironic that so many of its citizens are not only poor, but homeless as well. Like racism, homelessness is a social problem that we ignore only at the risk of injuring our own health and well-being.

Possible Solutions

It is easier to talk about ways to solve the homeless problem than it is to actually do something about it. A major difficulty in helping the homeless is that we do not know enough about them and their needs to bring about the best solutions.

Many political, civic and social groups think they know what needs to be done, but they often cannot agree on how to accomplish their goals or how to pay for them. One of the most important things we can do for the homeless is to help find them good jobs. A "good" job will pay enough money for a person to live above the poverty level. He or she can then afford to rent a comfortable apartment, buy groceries, and pay utility bills. A good job also gives a person dignity and a feeling of participating in society. With a decent-paying job, a person has a sense of control in his or her life, and hope for a better future.

But providing good jobs is easier said than done. In recent years, the job market has undergone dramatic changes. We have seen how unemployed steelworkers cannot find a job for which they have been trained. Also, such technological advances as automation, computerized information services and robotics have eliminated the need for many human workers in certain job markets. Job-training and other educational opportunities are needed to help teach new skills to those who cannot find employment without them. Even with the added cost of job training, putting homeless people to work is still the cheapest and best solution to their problems. When the lives of individual homeless people are improved, they will begin to take responsibility for themselves.

Another solution to homelessness is to build low-income housing that poor people can afford. This solution is built into the very word "homelessness." The only cure for homelessness is to ensure that all people have access to a place they can call their own. Government knows this will cost a lot of tax money, but, on the other hand, the construction process would create jobs and put more people to work. Moreover, if jobs go hand-in-hand with low-income housing, the cost to taxpayers will be much less because a rise in employment will increase tax revenues.

The need for housing and jobs is one thing, getting them is another. The same is true for the dilemma of those homeless people who are unable to take care of themselves. With proper community support and resources, many homeless people with mental illnesses could become useful members of society. But without a place to live and with no way of finding and holding a job, they are left to wander homeless in the streets. One solution would be to build community homes that people with mental problems could turn to for help. Putting mentally ill people who are not dangerous

A familiar way to keep warm on the street is to sleep on a
steam grate, like this one in Philadelphia.

behind hospital walls doesn't always work. For one
thing, government hospitals are already full to capaci-
ty. For another, these people do not want to go there.
Given a choice between life on the streets and life in a
mental hospital, these homeless people will usually

choose the streets.

Ed Koch, former mayor of New York City, found this out a few years ago. He was frustrated by the number of homeless people living miserably—sometimes dying—in the winter streets. He wanted to do something about their situation. He ordered health department officials to round up mentally ill homeless people and put them in hospitals for their own health and safety. But they refused to go. They knew what life in a hospital was like. Eventually, after a court battle, they were allowed to stay in the streets.

What about women and children who cannot work? A homeless woman with children needs some form of inexpensive child care before she can take a job. State and federal governments currently do very little in the way of supporting low-income child care centers. The costs of private child care centers are so high that only people who have well-paying jobs can afford them.

All of these possible solutions to homelessness are expensive. However, when considering the immediate cost in tax dollars, people often overlook the long-term rewards. For example, many homeless people who receive moral and economic support can once again become productive members of society.

The ultimate goal in eliminating homelessness is to give everyone the chance to live a meaningful life. The homeless need to be able to help themselves again, to feel good about who they are and what they can accomplish. An example of this is found when homeless people take over abandoned buildings, fix them up, and live in them. These "squatters" work to help themselves. They repair the plumbing and rewire the electricity. They clean up the buildings as best they can with the little they have. But their biggest problem is that the government owns many of the empty buildings they occupy. Therefore these people are trespassing, which is against the law. Another hazard is that many of these old buildings are condemned for safety reasons and can be dangerous. If someone gets hurt,

I Ain't Got No Home

Words and Music by Woody Guthrie

I ain't got no home, I'm just a-roamin' 'round,
Just a wand'rin' worker, I go from town to town.
And the police make it hard wherever I may go,
And I ain't got no home in this world any more.

My brothers and my sisters are stranded on this
    road,
A hot, dusty road that a million feet have trod.
Rich man took my home and drove me from my
    door,
And I ain't got no home in this world any more.

Was a farmin' on the shares and always I was poor,
My crops I laid into the banker's store.
And my wife took down and died up on the cabin
    floor,
And I ain't got no home in this world any more.

Now I just ramble 'round to see what I can see,
This wide, wicked world is a funny place to be.
The gambling man is rich and the working man is
    poor,
And I ain't got no home in this world any more.

the government could be sued. So even though these homeless are trying, they are putting themselves in further jeopardy.

Yet little has been done to help restore the many abandoned and fire-damaged buildings in America's cities. A program to do so would provide both jobs and housing. During the Great Depression, President Roosevelt created the Civilian Conservation Corps and the Work Project Administration. These were programs that put unemployed people to work doing useful things such as building roads for our National Parks. The homeless could do many things for themselves and their communities, if given a chance. They could landscape vacant lots to make playgrounds, paint old buildings, help to repair roads and bridges. Maybe they could even restore entire city blocks, building homes to live in. This kind of effort on the part of the government could work again.

Conclusions

Homelessness may be a fact of human life, but in a rich country such as the United States there is truly no excuse for it. Yet it will be hard to help homeless people completely until we know more about them and how many there are. It is hoped that the 1990 Census, which attempted to count *all* the homeless, will be a good beginning. We must also learn more about their lives. Without this kind of information we cannot offer adequate programs to provide moral and economic support.

Homelessness is an affliction of our society. Homelessness damages not only individuals, but the country as a whole. There are many reasons for homelessness. It is important to remember that the problem in America today was not created by the homeless themselves. We should also remember that of all our fellow human beings, the homeless are among the very least of us.

Glossary

ADVOCATES. One who defends or vindicates a cause. Advocates for the homeless are people and organizations who work to improve the quality of life for the homeless, and who lobby for government action to solve the problem of homelessness.

BABY BOOMERS. The generation of Americans born between 1946 and the mid-1960s.

CENSUS. The survey of the United States population, once every ten years, as mandated by the Constitution.

EVICTED. When a person or family is legally forced to move out of their residence.

FOOD STAMPS. The U.S. government program that supplements a family's income with coupons redeemable for food at any store.

INTACT FAMILY. A family that is not separated; an intact homeless family may live together in a car or tent, for example.

STANDARD OF LIVING. The economic level that a family is accustomed to, measured by family income, the cost of shelter and other necessities, and what, if any, money is left over each month.

UNEMPLOYMENT. Adults without jobs are *unemployed,* periodically the U.S. government surveys the number of people in America who are unemployed.

Bibliography

Books

Kozol, Jonathan. *Rachel and Her Children*. New York: Crown Publishers, 1988

Magazines And Newspapers

Coles, Robert. "Lost Youth." *Vogue*, July 1989: 186

Dobbin, Muriel. "The Children of the Homeless." *U.S. News & World Report*, August 3, 1987: 20

Filer, Randall K. "What We Really Know About the Homeless." *The Wall Street Journal*, April 10, 1990: 18

Futrell, Mary Hatwood. "A Cruel Catch-22: Homeless Children Without Education." *NEA Today*, April 1988: 2

"History's Losers: 14 Million Refugees." *World Press Review*, November 1989: 14

King, Patricia. "A Family Down and Out." *Newsweek*, January 12, 1987: 44-46

Leslie, Connie. "Can A Shelter Be a School? Some Children Don't Have a Home or a Classroom." *Newsweek*, January 23, 1989: 51

Plummer, William. "Lashanda Daniels's Outstanding Essay on the Homeless Was No Academic Exercise—She'd Been There." *People Weekly*, July 31, 1989: 39

Rubin, Nancy. "American's New Homeless." *McCall's*, November 1988: 118

Settle, Mel. "Must We Tear Them Down? How Urban Renewal Contributes to Homelessness," *The Humanist*, May-June 1989: 9

Whitman, David. "Who's Who Among the Homeless: A Guide to Life on the Streets." *The New Republic*, June 6, 1988: 18

Wright, James D. "The Worthy and Unworthy Homeless." *Society*, July-August 1988: 64

Index

Picture Credits